Faith Talk

CONTENTS

Published by Christian Board of Publication, St. Louis, Missouri
Writer: Sandra Messick   Art Director: Michael A. Domínguez
Editor: Michael E. Dixon   Cover design: Michael Foley
Series Editor: Michael E. Dixon   Interior design: Arista Graphics and Elizabeth Wright

Printed in the United States of America.

O9-BHL-279

Visit our Web site: www.cbp21.com

WELCOME TO FAITH TALK

IF...

you are saying, "Help! I'm a leader! What do I do next?" go to pages 5-8.

you are already a Christian and want to be more comfortable sharing your faith with others, read the article "Guides to a Great Adventure." It begins on page 9.

you want to schedule the leaders and locations for this study, turn to page 13.

you're getting ready for the first meeting of your Faith Crossings group and want to read Session 1 before you get there (always a good idea), it begins on page 14.

you want to discover unique activities to add to your Faith Crossings experience, check out "Enriching the Experience" on page 76.

you have a difficult time finding you way around in the Bible, read "A Quick Bible Road Map," on page 78.

FAITH TALK

AN INTRODUCTION

As we grow within our faith, we sometimes find ourselves struggling with God. We ask questions to which there are no simple answers. *Where did I come from? Why am I here? Who is God? Why do bad things happen to good people? What is the relationship of Jesus Christ to God? How do I make sense of the Spirit? Can I trust the words of the Bible?* These questions are natural and expected as we move forward in our journey of faith. And yet, these same questions can cause the most learned theologians and church leaders to stutter and stammer their way to an answer. If those with years of training can't find simple answers, what hope do we have?

Maybe we shouldn't look for simple answers, but instead, struggle with the questions of faith, and embrace the struggle. In Genesis, the first book of the Bible, we discover a story about a man named Jacob who wrestled in the darkness with a mysterious being. Earlier, Jacob had been wrestling with his own fears and conscience. He was traveling back to try to reconcile himself with his family, especially his angry brother Esau, whom he had swindled many years before. Late one evening he separated himself from the others and met a stranger. The story tells us that "a man wrestled with him until daybreak." As the sun began to rise, Jacob was winning the struggle. The man, or angel, struck Jacob in the hip, causing him to forever limp. Jacob, ever stubborn and determined, held fast to his opponent and asked for a blessing before he released his opponent. The man responded that from that day on Jacob would be known as Israel, "for you have striven with God and with humans, and have prevailed" (Genesis 32:28). That name, born in struggle, became the name of a people. This people, in some ways, continued the struggle, seeking the blessing of God.

Our hope lies in the God of Jacob. Like Jacob, we, too, struggle with our faith and the direction God would have us to go. And like Jacob, it is in the midst of the struggle that we are blessed.

Faith Talk asks the tough questions of our faith, but it doesn't provide simple solutions. The plain truth is, there are no simple answers to these faith questions. Instead, this material offers points of struggle, places to begin the questioning process, and directions for finding answers. As individuals and within the group, it is hoped that you will resolve some of the questions, be able to live with those that have no ready answers, and most of all, find the blessing that comes from wrestling with God.

Some in this small group study might be people who are still seeking, who are looking at Christianity as an option. Others might be returning to an active faith for the first time in several years. Others might be in the early stages of faith and membership. Others may be longtime Christians who want to take a fresh look at their basic beliefs. Wherever you are on your faith journey, we wish you God's blessing. Listen to one another. Trust one another. Speak openly. Don't judge. Pray for one another. Be alert to the possibilities that God's spirit may be present in your midst.

IS IT MY TURN TO LEAD?

By Cathy Myers Wirt

Remember these leadership tips:

- ✓ **Read** the lesson more than once before leading it.
- ✓ Allow enough time to **gather materials or resources** you may need.
- ✓ **Pray** for the group members by name during the week.
- ✓ Create a **spirit of hospitality** and welcome in the meeting space through decoration, refreshments (if appropriate to your time), name tags if needed.
- ✓ Offer brief gathering times for quick **sharing of news** of the congregation/group.
- ✓ If sensitive topics arise, agree on a policy of **confidentiality.** Stories told in a group should be shared outside of the group only when permission has been given.
- ✓ **Take all questions seriously** as a sign of the respect we hold for one another.
- ✓ If a person in the group has had a **tragedy** during the week, take time to deal with it even if it means delaying the session.
- ✓ **Direct** persons with serious emotional or spiritual dilemmas to the pastor.
- ✓ **Call persons who are absent** from the group during the week to check in on them and let them know that they have been missed.
- ✓ Encourage group members to **invite new people** to the group.
- ✓ **Ask for help** when you come across a topic or a problem in a group. You don't have to do this alone!
- ✓ **Allow silence** in the group while people think. Don't jump in too quickly to fill the quiet.
- ✓ Start and end the group with a **time of prayer.**
- ✓ Begin and end the session **on time.**

✓ **Vary your leading style** between thoughtful discussion, activity, and visual/auditory experiences. People learn in different ways.

✓ Connect the life of the group to the **congregation and the wider church.**

✓ **Watch the news media** for examples of the topics you are studying and bring in the articles for discussion and prayer.

✓ **Thank God** for the learning you are enjoying by leading the group. Leadership is one of the best ways to learn and increase your own faith.

✓ **Don't assume** that the people in the room know each other well.

✓ **Don't argue.** When strongly different opinions are expressed, try to avoid a win/lose style of discussion.

✓ **Invite but don't coerce people to discuss.** Some people learn by listening and may be fully attentive without speaking.

✓ Help keep one from **monopolizing the discussion.** Pass the discussion to another person by saying, "[name], what do you think about this idea/story?" Try always to do this in love.

✓ **Avoid getting sidetracked** by talking about people not in the room. Try to keep the discussion about the experiences and ideas of those in the room.

✓ **Avoid becoming unfocused** on the session. A group that has spun into other topics can be brought back by statements like "What in the session reminded you of that?" or "Wow, how did we get to this topic from today's lesson?" or "What you just said reminded me about our lesson today because…."

RACING THE CLOCK

A Leader's Guide to Getting through a Session

A typical FAITH CROSSINGS session gives more activities than time may allow. That's good news—there's a lot to choose from; and bad news—how do you choose? That depends. When you're leading a group of adults, there are a lot of variables! An activity that may take five minutes for one group may lead to a twenty-minute discussion in another. With all that in mind, here are some suggestions.

- Encourage everyone to read "Before the Session" before arriving. This section provides continuity and background to help the group members start "on the same page." Then the leader doesn't have to take time to summarize the information.

- In most cases, each session has four basic movements, each beginning with the phrase "Connecting with…" Be sure that you spend some time with each movement. (See the paragraph below on how to adapt this flow to a forty-five-minute church school session.)

- Note the key activities. 🔑 This logo after the title of an activity is your clue that it is essential to the session. If you don't have enough time to cover everything, be sure you cover the key activities.

- Pick and choose from the remaining activities, according to your interests and the interests of the group. If your group doesn't like an arts-based activity, for example, that may be a good one to draw a big X through before the session even begins.

- Go with the flow. Don't let agenda anxiety put a premature end to a really great discussion. And don't drag out an activity that people aren't responding to—just summarize and move on.

Adapting to a church school setting

Each session is written for a ninety-minute group setting. If you want to use it in church school, how do you adapt? Two suggestions:

1. Allow twelve weeks for the six sessions. During the first week of a given session, cover what you can and close with a prayer. When the next week's session begins, summarize what the group covered the first week. Then work through the remaining activities.

2. Lead one session a week for six weeks. If you do this, there will probably be time for little more than the key activities. Highlight some of the important discussion questions you wish to include from the other activities. Encourage the group members to read the whole session, but select those activities for group use that connect to your particular group.

GUIDES TO A GREAT ADVENTURE

By Robert W. Pierce

Yesterday was bright and sunny at 30,000 feet over the Grand Canyon. On the flight from Los Angeles toward home in Indianapolis, the plane paralleled the great canyon's rim for the full length of this masterpiece of nature. Seeing the canyon reminded me of hikes and trails and adventures into unfamiliar areas, and how important it is to have a guide, someone who has been there and knows the way.

You've needed a guide at various times, haven't you? Remember the directions you asked for when you were unsure of streets and intersections, or when you sought advice on a big decision that had to be made? Guides are very important.

A helpful guide, we hope, speaks out of experience and wisdom, is credible, and gives understandable information.

Guess what! Being a "Good News Guide," a faith guide, is very similar. When the Ethiopian court official, reading the prophet Isaiah, heard Phillip ask: "Do you understand what you are reading?" he responded: "How can I, unless someone guides me?" (Acts 8:26–40). Faith sharing is relational;

- ▲ it's one person listening to the need of another,
- ▲ relating that need to something in his or her own faith experience,
- ▲ putting the information or insight into understandable words, and
- ▲ sharing it in love and grace. Guiding.

To share faith "relationally" is certainly less threatening than the old styles of evangelism that encouraged rather impersonal efforts, such as knocking on strangers' doors or handing out flyers on street corners. Just think of the ongoing relationships you have right now, relationships with people who are not going to church or are not convinced that faith in Christ is important. You already know them through a variety of ways: PTA, social gatherings, athletics, community service organizations, and the list goes on. Some level of friendship is already established, maybe even some level of trust. And sometimes they might even ask your advice—your guidance—on some special issue or topic in their lives. It's at those "guidance moments," those often-missed opportunities, that you and I can bring our own faith experience to bear on our friend's dilemma. This is not "hard-sell" evangelism; this is one friend giving another friend information or hope or encouragement that has as its basis the good news of God's activity in our own lives.

I think it's pretty apparent, though, that you can't be a very helpful guide if you don't know what you're talking about. I don't want someone telling me how to climb a rock wall of the Grand Canyon who hasn't done it already. I don't need theory; I need information or wisdom based on experience. So, the prior step to relational faith sharing—being a faith guide for someone else—is to be sure that you are grounded in faith, yourself. One blind guide leading another spells trouble.

The old saying is "You can't give what you don't have"; so if I am to be an effective faith guide, I have to be sure my own faith house is in order. The insights and wisdom of the Holy Spirit come through us only to the extent that we are tuned into prayer, meaningful worship, scriptural study and reflection, and other spiritual adventures. I know lots of people who have the hearts and wills to help their friends, a desire based on rather tenuous faith connections, but they are unable because the depth of their own faith development is too shallow.

If you want God to make you an instrument of good news and hope, then God's good news and hope have to be alive in your life—and you have to be able to articulate that hope. You probably know the old story of the travelers who stopped an old farmer on a country road and asked directions to a nearby town. The old-timer started out by pointing off in one direction and suggesting roads to follow, then said, "No, maybe this is better..." but having gotten a few sentences into the new directions, he stammered and pointed toward a third alternative. Frustrated, he finally gave up, saying, "Well, I guess you just can't get there from here!" If you can't put the directions into understandable words, if you can't tell your faith story when the opportunity suddenly appears, then the guidance is of no use at all.

Relational faith sharing is possible only when you have reflected on God's activity in your own life and formulated that God experience into a concise, concrete, credible story—one that can be understood by the least faithful or the most skeptical. Ask yourself: "What difference does believing in Jesus Christ make in my own life? How does faith impact my daily life? Of what value is the church in my experience?" Answer those questions, reflect prayerfully on the answers, and you're on the way to a story to tell when the moment comes.

Another very important aspect of faith sharing is simple listening.

Imagine standing on a street corner, being tapped on the shoulder by a stranger who says: "Let me tell you how to get to Montgomery, Alabama." What? I don't want to know that—I don't need to know. Who are you to presume that I need or want your guidance, unless I ask for it? Sometimes heavy-handed faith sharing scares people away from God. That's the kind of faith sharing that assumes it has the right doctrinal answer, the only interpretation, the final word on faith—and gives you the full load whether you want it or not. That kind of faith sharing proposes that it has the answers even though you haven't asked the questions.

That kind of faith sharing doesn't listen. But helpful faith sharing always responds to the life issues arising in spontaneous conversations or encounters, those special Holy Spirit moments when life and faith intersect. For example: When you are sitting with your friend in the locker room after a workout and she says: "I just feel sometimes that I don't have a grip on life anymore. Things just seem so out of balance these days." In that moment, you are standing at the intersection of a life dilemma and a spiritual opportunity. As you hear the pain or despair or frustration of your friend, think to yourself: How does faith speak to her need? What can I offer out of my own faith experience that will be good news in this moment? What story can I tell from my faith journey that will be relevant, helpful, and hopeful for my friend?

The final thought is, perhaps, the most important one. Having reflected on your own faith experience so that you feel comfortable and confident in sharing it, having been a good listener to the needs of your friends and relating those needs to the good news of Jesus Christ, having let God's love come through you in a caring, supportive response, and having accepted the joy of being a Good News Guide—the rest is up to the Holy Spirit.

So, you see, evangelism isn't scary or old fashioned. It's one friend telling another very good news—all empowered and prompted by the Holy Spirit.

Roger Pierce is Vice President, Homeland Ministries Center for Congregational Growth and Vitality, Christian Church (Disciples of Christ).

WHEN FAITH CROSSINGS HAPPEN

Our life experiences and our faith often cross paths. We come to moments when we need our faith to help us interpret the meaning of our life experiences and to make Christian choices. Or our life experiences cause us to rethink our beliefs. When we come to such crossing points between faith and daily life, our lives change.

 Faith crossings happen when people share their beliefs lovingly and honestly, in a context of faith and love. The way other people live out and express their faith shapes our own. A Christian, small group setting creates a context for this to happen. We become pilgrims together on a faith journey. Every FAITH CROSSINGS session promotes this interaction with activities under this heading and icon: **Connecting with one another.**

 Faith crossings happen when we open ourselves to new discoveries about life and faith. Whether its in reading the Bible or the daily news, downloading from the Internet or watching television, we receive new information that helps shape our understanding. Every FAITH CROSSINGS session promotes new learning with activities under this heading and icon: **Connecting with the theme.**

 Faith crossings happen when we decide what to do next. How do our faith and experiences lead us to change the course of our daily lives? Toward what actions do our faith crossings prod us? Every FAITH CROSSINGS session promotes this decision making with activities under this heading and icon: **Connecting with life.**

 Faith crossings happen when we celebrate God's presence in our midst. God calls us to respond, to praise, to pray, to worship, to love. Every FAITH CROSSINGS session promotes worship and reflection with activities under this heading and icon: **Connecting with God.**

SESSION SCHEDULE

Session 1
When _____ Leader _____
Where _____

Session 2
When _____ Leader _____
Where _____

Session 3
When _____ Leader _____
Where _____

Session 4
When _____ Leader _____
Where _____

Session 5
When _____ Leader _____
Where _____

Session 6
When _____ Leader _____
Where _____

Special Activities
When _____ Leader _____
Where _____

1

Who Are We and Why Are We Here?

Session Focus: We begin with the human question. What is the meaning and direction of our lives? What is our nature and how do we deal with the ambiguities of life? What is it that draws us to look for something beyond ourselves, that makes us always seekers and travelers?

Scriptures used: Genesis 1—2; Psalm 8

BEFORE THE SESSION

Read and reflect on this introduction. Consider the questions that have arisen in your life as you have attempted to make meaning out of your world.

From the instant they are born, infants begin the process of meaning making. From the variety of stimuli surrounding them, they begin to sort out and categorize their environment. They learn that the breast or bottle eases their hunger. They learn that certain people are constant and can be trusted. Later, they begin to make the connection between crying out a request and having a need fulfilled. They have begun to make sense of their world. This process will continue for the rest of their lives!

As we grow, we humans continue to try to make meaning of our lives. Early on we sort through differences between hunger and satisfaction, light/day and dark/night. We may answer the questions of how to keep warm when we are cold and how to find drink when we are thirsty, but the need to make sense of our world continues.

If we are in a secure environment, the questions shift from meeting physical needs to meeting emotional, intellectual, and spiritual needs. We may no longer need to sort out how to appease hunger, but we may still hunger for answers to life's basic questions. Why are we here? How did we get here? What is the meaning and purpose of our being? These questions arise in different forms throughout our lives. Teenagers may struggle with their place among peers or within their families. The awkwardness and self-consciousness of the age may cause them to question whether they will ever fit in! People in their thirties or forties may find themselves questioning values and roles in the midst of a midlife crisis. How did I get to this point? Is this the direction I am called to be traveling? What am I supposed to do with my life? These questions may arise even in the midst of an outwardly successful career and life. A person nearing the end of life's journey may be wondering if this is all there is to life, and what happens now. It is human nature to seek out not only an existence, but also a reason for existence. It is not enough just to live. We need to make or discover meaning in our life.

Who are we? How did we get here and why? What is our purpose in living? Obviously, we can look at such questions from many different perspectives. We will look at them from the perspective of Christian faith.

1. Meet one another

Every small group has its own chemistry. As members learn to trust one another and to be responsible for one another's trust, community can grow. To help build that community, complete two or more of the sentence stems below, read them to the others, and explain a little bit about your answer.

Allow a few moments for introductions. Describe the general nature of the course and what your hopes are for it. Invite others to say what they hope will happen during the small group experience, as well.

▲ When I was in high school, others thought of me as….

▲ If time and money were no object, I would travel to….

▲ If I had all the qualifications, I would love to work as a….

▲ If I could sit down for dinner with any three people from history, I would dine with….

▲ A personality trait that I'd like to develop is….

▲ When I was a child, my hero/heroine was….

▲ Ten years from now I'd like to….

2. Recall some questions of childhood

Some of life's hardest-to-answer questions are asked by children. "Why did God make mosquitoes?" "Why is the sky blue?" "Why do I have to eat my carrots?" What such questions do you recall? Think about questions you may have asked as a child, or questions you have heard children ask. How did others respond to the questions? What answers were given (if any)?

3. Name life's questions

Futility seems to be a universal human feeling and experience. Think of times, especially in the past week, when you experienced a sense of futility.

Begin with light-hearted moments. When does it seem that you are spinning your wheels and getting nowhere? Perhaps you struggle with the "in" basket that never gets empty, or the students or employees who ask the same questions over and over again. Talk about these memories with the group. See how many you can list.

Now, turn to more serious feelings of futility. Perhaps never-ending bills, stagnating relationships, or chronic or terminal illnesses trigger such feelings. Listen carefully and prayerfully as members identify some of life's

Discuss together.

struggles. Remember that what seems obvious to one may be an incredible struggle for another. This is a time for listening and affirming, not problem-solving. After each person has had the opportunity to participate, pray briefly, thanking God for each individual and for God's presence in the midst of struggle.

After praying together, briefly identify together the questions raised by such feelings. Some may be Why? Why me? Why now? Is this all there is to life? These are heartfelt, human questions that all of us raise at one time or another. At the root of each question is another: What is the meaning and purpose of my life? To put it another way: For what purpose was I created?

4. Start at the beginning

The Bible as we know it actually contains not one but two stories about how the world began. They are read as one unit so often that it is easy to miss where one ends and the second begins. The first story is found in Genesis 1:1—2:3. The second story picks up at Genesis 2:4 and continues to the end of chapter 3. Many Bible scholars believe these stories were written at different times by different authors for different reasons. An anonymous editor joined them together at a still later date. Read the stories. How are they alike? How are they different? What do you notice about them that you might have missed before? It may be helpful to outline them side-by-side on paper, chalkboard, or newsprint.

Creation stories are written or told to answer the basic human questions of where we came from, how we got here, and why. How do these stories answer these questions? Who was the creator? In what order were things created? How was humankind created? For what purpose? What other questions are answered? How do they attempt to explain how the world works? Many different cultures have creation stories.

CONNECTING WITH THE THEME

Read and discuss Genesis 1—2. If the group is large, divide into teams to analyze each story.

Have half the group read one story, the other half the other. Then ask each group to paraphrase its account.

5. Look for meaning

It's easy to get sidetracked while discussing this topic. The purpose isn't to argue the scientific validity of the Bible, but to explore its faith claims.

Discuss.

Western scientific culture, of course, has its own stories of creation. They focus on the process of creation—how things happened. Creation stories such as those in Genesis were written to answer different questions—why things happened. The Genesis stories make a faith claim that the creative processes of the universe are ultimately the work of a loving, creative God.

For many Christians, the issue at hand when comparing the creation stories of Genesis to scientific accounts of creation isn't in the timing or the order of events. The issue, rather, is whether there is an ultimate reason or purpose for creation and for our existence as human beings. Is the world (and our place in it) a cosmic coincidence, or part of a purposeful design from a loving God?

From your own perspective, what evidence do you see that life is a cosmic coincidence? that it is a gift of God? How does either position influence the way we look at the world? How does either position influence the way we act and make decisions?

6. Reflect upon being made in God's image 🔑

Creation stories help us make meaning out of our world and understand our place in it. We may have been created to do something specific (care for the earth, for example) or for no particular reason. How does that give us direction in life? In answering the question of where we come from and why, we also begin to answer the question of what to make of our lives.

According to the Genesis stories, we were created in God's image, to be company for God and one another. What difference does it make in our lives to realize that we are the image of God?

To be made in God's image doesn't mean that we are little gods. It does mean that we are like God in some significant ways. It means that we can have relationship with God and with one another. Look back at the Genesis stories again. What do they say about God? What does that imply about what it may mean to be made in God's image? (For example, God declared all that was created "good." What does that say about our ability to value the world and other people around us?)

What in the Genesis stories points to the idea that God deeply desires a relationship with the universe and with people, and that God created us to live in relationship—with nature, with others, and with God? What in our own experience of life points us to this idea?

In Genesis 3, we have an account of the origins of sin. Interestingly enough, when sin happens, the relationship between God and the humans is damaged. What did the humans do that damaged the relationship? How do similar actions damage relationships today—with God or with other people? We often think of sin as breaking laws. What happens when we think of it as breaking relationships? What does this concept add to our understanding of who we are as human beings?

7. Write your own story

As a group, or as individuals, create a story that offers an answer to the questions "Who are we?" and "Why are we here?" This can take many different forms—a creation story, a parable, a fable, a dialogue, or a poem. What questions will it attempt to answer? What questions will it leave unanswered? Why was humankind given life? by whom? for what purpose? When the stories are completed, have a storytelling session around an imaginary campfire.

8. Create a cartoon or skit

In the Peanuts cartoons, Lucy offers psychiatric advice to the world for a five-cent fee. Imagine that

Ask if anyone recalls what happened next in the Genesis story. If no one does, give hints about the fruit tree and the snake, or be prepared to summarize the story.

CONNECTING WITH LIFE

If people don't have time to complete their stories, encourage them to finish the stories later and tell them at the beginning of the next session.

For
Activity 8,
have the
group (or
teams) visual-
ize what
might happen
in this scene,
and either act
it out or
sketch it.

Lucy is sitting at her homemade psychiatrist's booth. Charlie Brown arrives seeking help. In the first frame he says, "I'm having trouble with the meaning of life. Why am I here? What is it all about?" Complete the cartoon. What will Lucy say? How will Charlie Brown respond? How would you answer his questions?

9. Respond to a question

In the 1997 movie "As Good as it Gets," actor Jack Nicholson asks a group of patients in a psychiatrist's waiting room, "What if this is as good as it gets?" How would you respond? What answers might the patients give to such a question? What was the character really asking or saying with his question?

10. Sum it up

"Who are we?" "Why are we here?" Philosophers, theologians, other scholars, and millions of other people have reflected on these questions in one way or another. There is no single answer that everyone can agree upon. Our cultural background and values, our family traditions, our belief systems, and our life experiences all shape what we bring to the questions. Christians and non-Christians have fundamentally different responses to these questions.

What is your response to these questions, based upon your reflections on Genesis 1—3, your own experiences and beliefs, and the discussions you have had in this session? What does Christian belief bring to your understanding of the question and your response to it? If you are not a Christian, what is attractive and what raises questions about a Christian response to the questions that this session is based upon?

As we grow, develop, and grapple with life's experiences, our responses to life's basic questions can change. (Some say that they *have* to change, if we are to be honest with ourselves.) How has your response to these questions changed over the last few years or over the

Invite group
members to give
their responses.

Don't be frustrated
if this session
doesn't come up
with any clear and
straightforward
answers to the
questions. Affirm
that we are always
on a journey seek-
ing provisional
answers, but
that we are on the
journey together.

Faith Talk

course of your life? In what direction are you moving if you are "between answers"?

If the group has little experience finding things in the Bible, refer to the article "A Quick Bible Road Map" on page 78.

Set a mood for worship, perhaps by lighting a candle and playing reflective music. Invite people to close their eyes and listen prayerfully as one person reads the prayer aloud.

11. Reflect upon a psalm of praise

Find Psalm 8. Read it aloud. Discuss briefly how this psalm functions as a creation story. What questions does it answer? What questions does it raise? Remember that it was written as a hymn to God. What were the feelings of the writer? What feelings do you feel as you think about creation and your part within it?

12. Read a contemporary prayer

The following prayer by David R. Grant[1] is based upon Psalm 8. Let your "wise child within" reflect on the mystery of what it means to be someone that God loves.

Sovereign Lord,

> *we listen for the wise child within,*
> *who still wonders at your glory*
> > *beyond the glory we see in the heavens.*

We marvel and long for that early innocence
> *incapable of cultivating enemies within and*
> *adversaries without.*

We yearn to recapture juvenile surprise and astonishment
> *at the grandeur of your days*
> *and the splendor of your nights.*

> *Yellowed moon casting silver shadow,*
> *a milky way splayed against dark sky,*
> *pinpricks of brilliance varying in intensity,*
> *twinkling distances beyond imagination,*
> *time delayed but present.*

Sovereign Lord,
> *who encompasses every dimension*

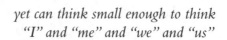

yet can think small enough to think
"I" and "me" and "we" and "us"

you draw us up to angel status
and graciously give us privilege and responsibility
to co-convene as guardians of the earth,
and labor for a just sustaining of life,
and a fair distribution of earth's means.

Sovereign Lord, Father, Son and Spirit,
creator, created, creating,
create a willing spirit in us, we pray.

In the name of the One who speaks for creation,
AMEN.

If the group is able and willing, sing a creation hymn together. Otherwise, simply say them together as a closing and benediction to the session.

13. Sing a hymn

Sing or say a hymn together that praises God for creation. Some suggestions: "For the Beauty of the Earth," "We Sing Your Mighty Power, O God," or "How Great Thou Art."

Looking ahead: Sessions 2, 4, and 5 suggest making banners as a visual way of communicating about God, Christ, and the Holy Spirit. Find out today if this is something that the group would like to try so you can gather any supplies needed.

---

[1]David R. Grant, *Grant Us your Peace: Prayers from Lectionary Psalms* (St. Louis, Chalice Press, 1998). Used by permission.

NOTES

2

God? Are You There?

Session Focus: What are some of the different ways people perceive God? Do we see God as a person, a cosmic force, a way of explaining things we haven't come to understand yet, a judge, a parent, or what? What are some images of God from the Bible, and how do they connect with our present world?

Scriptures Used: Exodus 3:13–14; Psalm 23; Isaiah 42:13–14; 49:14–15; 64:8; Matthew 6:9–13; 18:23–35; 22:1–14; 25:14–30; Luke 15:8–10; 1 John 4:8

BEFORE THE SESSION

Read and reflect in preparation for this session.

A tale is told of three people who were blind, as they encountered an elephant for the first time. Using their hands for sight, the three felt the animal and then described the images created in their minds. The first, feeling the trunk of the elephant, declared, "Elephants are like snakes, long and thin." The second, feeling the side of the elephant, declared, "Elephants are like walls, flat and high and wide." The third, wrapping his arms around one of the elephant's legs, declared, "Elephants are like trees, so thick one can hardly reach around them." Which one of the three was right? Which one was wrong? The answer, of course, is that they were all right, and they were all wrong. Their images were accurate as far as they went, but the images were incomplete. They didn't tell the whole story.

Faith Talk

The same is true of our image of God. Different people have different names for God. Each name conjures up a different picture of God. Names for God are revealed to us through scripture, church tradition, even in the music we sing. Yet all of the names put together still don't describe all that God is.

1. Name ourselves

Read and reflect as a group, or in small groups.

Open with a brief prayer, thanking God for each individual within the group. If you know each other fairly well, offer a specific thank-you for traits or gifts of each individual. (Example: Thank you for Linda's sense of humor. Thank you for Hector's knowledge of scripture.)

Then, consider the following questions. By how many names are you known? Think of the many different roles you play. Mother/Father? Sister/Brother? Parent? Adult child? Church leader? New Christian? Businessperson? Student? List as many as you can think of. It's probably more than you might at first imagine. Read your list to others in your group. Did they have any that also apply to you? Each of us has numerous roles that we carefully juggle each day of our lives. At different times, one role may take precedence over others, but we are still all of these roles—and more.

Now think of all of the names you have been called. (Hopefully there are many more positive ones than negative, but consider the negative as well.) Do you have a nickname? Do you use your middle name? Did you keep your maiden name after marriage, or did you take your spouse's name? (Some men today are adopting their wife's maiden name as their own.) What did your parents call you? What does your significant other call you? Do you have a favorite pet name? Is there a name that sets your teeth on edge? Tell some of these stories within your group.

Now think of words that people use to describe you. Are you considered smart? funny? serious?

hard-working? Within the group, tell at least two descriptive names for each individual.

Finally, briefly reflect on this statement: "I am more than the sum of my parts." Do you agree or disagree? Why?

2. Ask questions of God

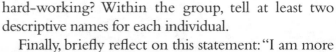

Imagine that you are a reporter and have been chosen to attend a press conference that God is holding! You have the opportunity to ask God a question. There are ground rules. The question has to be informational, not a request to do something. The question can't be about the future (no stock tips) or some secret of nature. It has to be about God. What question would you ask?

As you hear one another's questions, what questions do you think are answerable? If we were to do research on these questions, where might we find good sources?

3. Picture God

How do we envision God? By what name should God be called? Just as we as individuals have many names and play many roles, so God has many names and images. Of course, in Jewish and Christian belief, we know that God is a spirit, that God is invisible. To picture God as an old man with a beard, for example, is to limit God. To limit our concept of God to any image is to worship an idol. Yet we do often think in pictures, and visual images do come to mind when we think of God.

Fold a sheet of paper in half. On one half, draw a picture of God (or write a few words describing God) as you imagined in your childhood. On the other half, draw an image (or write a poem or paragraph) of God as you imagine today. Discuss together: How has the image changed over time? Where did the image come from? Why and when did it change, if it did?

Invite responses.

CONNECTING WITH THE THEME

Provide a sheet of paper and a pen or pencil for each person.

Assign various scriptures to individuals or small groups. Pair up people who have different translations to get a wider variety of response. Have everyone report back to the group as a whole. Some scriptures to consider are: Genesis 14:22; Exodus 3:13–14; Psalm 23; Matthew 6:9–13; 1 John 4:8; Luke 15:8–10; Isaiah 42:13–14; 49:14–15; 64:8. List these names where all can see. Use whatever means are available to do this— newsprint, chalkboard, dry-erase, poster board, or large sheets of paper.

Supply hymnals.

4. Seek God's name in scripture

The Bible uses numerous names for God. Some appear over and over again. Others appear only rarely. Each different name conjures up a different image of God. The biblical writers carefully chose these images to convey something about the nature and being of God. Review some of the names used for God in scripture. What images do they bring to mind? What might the writer have been trying to tell us about God? Sometimes footnotes will give a clue, especially in study Bibles.

Which of these names come as a surprise? What images have you not considered before?

5. Seek God's name in hymns

Browse through a hymnal or songbook used within your congregation. What are some of the names used for God? What are some images used in singing about or to God? If you discover any new images, add them to the list.

6. Seek God's name in history

Throughout the history of the church, theologians and church leaders have struggled with naming God. They have filled reams of paper with words about and for God. At times, some of these words have been set down as statements of faith or creeds. These creeds have expressed the names and images of God recognized by certain faith communities. Some of these have become institutionalized within the church and have, in fact, become a part of our fabric of faith. Many churches today recite weekly the Apostles' Creed or the Nicene Creed. Both of these statements of faith were labored over and given life some 1,200–1,500 years ago or more. Other faith statements have arisen more recently, yet still they reflect the struggle over identifying and describing the nature of God. One of the most

Many Names for God

Most of the Old Testament was written in Hebrew, the New Testament in Greek. Biblical translations often combine several words from the original language into only one or a few words in the modern language. The predominant name for God in the Old Testament is sometimes transliterated *Yahweh*. This is the name that God used when appearing in the burning bush to Moses (Exodus 3:13–14). It seems to be a causative form of the verb "to be," saying that God creates everything there is.

El was the root of a series of earlier names for God. *El Elyon* meant "God Most High"; *El Shaddai* meant "God Almighty" or "God of the Heights." *Elohim* was a plural form, but Israel used it to refer to the one God.

Adonai was a title, not a name. It meant "Lord." Interestingly enough, the old translation of God's name found in the King James Version, "Jehovah," combined the consonants YHWH (Yahweh) with the vowels from Adonai. Why? The Hebrew alphabet didn't have vowels, but used markings under the letters to indicate vowel sounds. For the Jews, the divine name is too holy to pronounce. So when they read the text aloud, they substituted their word for Lord, Adonai, and the text provided the vowels to help them make the substitution.

The Bible uses many other images for God, some from nature, some from family life, some from war and politics. The rich variety of names helps remind us that God goes beyond description!

descriptive of God's activity is the Statement of Faith adopted by the United Church of Christ in 1959. It is presented here in its revised form, approved in 1981.[1] What images of God does it use? What actions, attributes, and gifts does God possess? Add these to the list begun in Activity 3.

Either read together as a group, or divide the statement into sections and have individuals peruse each section.

> *We believe in you, O God, Eternal Spirit,*
> *God of our Savior Jesus Christ and our God,*
> *and to your deeds we testify.*
>
> *You call the worlds into being,*
> *create persons in your own image*
> *and set before each one the ways of life and*
> *death.*

Faith Talk

You seek in holy love to save all people from
    aimlessness and sin.

You judge people and nations by your righteous
will declared through prophets and apostles.

In Jesus Christ, the man of Nazareth, our
    crucified and risen Savior,
    you have come to us
    and shared our common lot,
    conquering sin and death
    and reconciling the world to yourself.

You bestow upon us your Holy Spirit,
    creating and renewing the Church of Jesus
        Christ,
    binding in covenant faithful people of all ages,
    tongues and races.

You call us into your Church
    to accept the cost and joy of discipleship,
    to be your servants in the service of others,
    to proclaim the gospel to all the world,
    to resist the powers of evil,
    to share in Christ's baptism and eat at his
        table,
    to join him in his passion and victory.

You promise to all who trust you
    forgiveness of sins and fullness of grace,
    courage in the struggle for justice and peace,
    your presence in trial and rejoicing,
    and eternal life in your realm which has no
        end.

Blessing and honor, glory and power be unto you. Amen.

If time allows, consider other creeds or faith statements. What claims do they make about God's activity?

7. Think outside the box

A popular phrase in business today is the notion of

"thinking outside the box." The message is that in order to arrive at new solutions, we must imagine beyond what we have always done. The image you drew in Activity 3 is in a sense "God in a box." Look back over the other names or images of God listed earlier. What images challenge you the most? Why? With which are you uncomfortable? Why? How do the different images expand your image of God? How do they allow you to think outside the box? Why is it important to expand our view of God? Some of the images for God may have been feminine. How comfortable are you with using feminine imagery for God? What are the characteristics generally associated with God as Father? How about God as Mother? What are the limitations in using only one (either masculine or feminine)? How would it help us expand our image of God to use images or words of more than one gender in referring to God?

Remember the phrase from Activity 1, "I am more than the sum of my parts"? How does this phrase apply to God?

8. Reconcile different characteristics of God

Sometimes we perceive—and scriptures portray—God as a stern judge. Other times we perceive—and scriptures portray—God as gracious and forgiving.

Sometimes we perceive—and scriptures portray—God as all-powerful, in ultimate control of history. Other times we perceive—and scriptures portray—a God who allows humans to exercise free will.

Sometimes we perceive—and scriptures portray—God as holy, far removed from a sinful world. Other times we perceive—and scriptures portray—God as a close friend, caring for us all in the smallest details of our lives.

These concepts seem contradictory. Yet each of them

CONNECTING WITH LIFE

Read and discuss.

Read Matthew
18:23–35;
22:1–14; 25:14–30.

says something valid and true about God. For example, look at some of the parables Jesus told about God and the kingdom. How do you reconcile the gracious God with the harsh master depicted in these parables? One explanation for God's judgment is that while God is a God of grace and unlimited forgiveness, God also allows us to face the consequences of our actions. What do you think? What could Jesus have been trying to tell us in these parables?

List the three statements. Help the group look at each one individually. Encourage different viewpoints.

Look again at the three paradoxes mentioned above:

▲ God is gracious, but God judges.

▲ God is all–powerful, but God gives us free will.

▲ God is holy and distant, but God is close and personal.

In each set, one of those statements will likely be closer to your own understanding of God than the other. Which one in each set is closer? Why? Think about the statement in each set that you didn't choose. How do you understand it? What can you learn from it?

9. Respond to two statements

Read the following two quotations. How do they relate to your experience of God?

Reality itself is grounded in God, whose basic being is love. To be made in the image of God means that we cannot see anyone or anything else as it truly is without seeing as God sees, that is, through the lense of love. [2]

The cross reveals that the most enduring power in our lives is God's love. Love becomes the ultimate value that is presented in the cross. Nothing stops God from loving us. Car wrecks can't do it. Neither can car bombs. Getting fired from your job won't do it. Your husband's leaving after twenty-two years of marriage doesn't diminish God's love either. Your child's becoming a wandering homeless man and breaking your heart and rendering you sleepless night after night won't stop God's love from flowing toward you. [3]

10. Experience God's presence

In scripture, God spoke to humankind in a variety of ways. In the creation story (Genesis 2), God seems to speak directly to Adam and Eve. God is even portrayed as one who walks through the garden in the cool of the day. God called Moses through a burning bush to deliver the Hebrews from Egypt. God spoke in a whirlwind to answer the suffering Job's questions. God called to the prophet Elijah in a still, small voice. Prophets experienced God through visions; numerous people met God through the person of Jesus Christ. Saul, a man who persecuted Christians, encountered God in a vision while on the road to Damascus and became the apostle Paul. How does God speak today? How do you know when you have encountered God? What are some of the ways you encounter God? Through prayer? through worship? through others? Does God ever speak as openly and boldly today as God seemed to do in scripture? How can we be more open to encountering God? In what ways can we encourage God to speak to us and reveal Godself to us?

11. Write a faith statement

Divide the group into teams and invite them to create and discuss their statements.

Having thought about all the names for God and characteristics of God, what names are most meaningful to you? If you had to describe God's activity in the world, or in your own life, what would you say? Write a brief statement of faith. Begin with "I believe..." and then fill it in with four or five sentences about God's activity. Discuss your statements with others in your group. Without judging or critiquing, discuss the images presented in these statements. If possible, write a faith statement for the group as a whole. Use a consensus process to come to agreement about words and phrases. That is, carefully discuss differing views and opinions. Seek a win-win situation where everyone can accept, if not embrace, the images used. Try to avoid voting on names for God, thus setting up a win-lose scenario.

Keep in mind that all of these names give us glimpses of God's nature and being. Remember, too, that all of the images put together still do not completely reveal God to us. In the end, we are using human language to describe the divine—an impossible task!

12. Create a banner

As you continue this study, consider creating group banners using pictures and symbols that reflect the nature of God, Jesus, and the Holy Spirit. Consider sharing the banners with the congregation as a whole. In this session, begin with a banner dedicated to God. How will God be portrayed? What images will be used? Will you use words, pictures, or both? Which colors will you choose? fabrics? other materials? Be creative in the use of materials and images. Allow the banners to be a visual statement of faith reflecting the group's belief about the Trinity.

13. Read a litany

Praise to the God of Many Names

Creator God, we give you praise for the world you have made.

Mother God, we give you thanks for the life you have nurtured.

Father God, we give you praise for strengthening us daily.

Shepherd God, we give you thanks for a guiding hand and gentle leading.

Loving God, we give you praise for everlasting faithfulness.

Forgiving God, we give you thanks for one more chance, again and again.

Almighty and powerful, compassionate and caring, we praise you for the many ways you reveal yourself to us.

Rock and Redeemer, Hope and Sustainer, we thank you for the human words that attempt to

CONNECTING WITH GOD

If the group doesn't want to make banners, invite them to individually write sentence prayers that they can take with them as a reminder to pray.

Read together "Praise to the God of Many Names." One half of the group can read the regular type, the other the bold type. Close with a brief prayer.

know the divine. We thank you for the ways beyond words that you make yourself known.

May you grant us eyes to see, ears to hear, and hearts to perceive your presence.

May all blessing, honor and glory be yours. Amen.

[1] *United Church of Christ Statement of Faith* used by permission of the United Church of Christ, 700 Prospect Avenue, Cleveland, OH 44115.

[2] Roberta Bondi, *To Pray & To Love* (Philadelphia: Fortress Press, 1991), p. 36.

[3] R. Scott Colglazier, *Finding a Faith That Makes Sense* (St. Louis: Chalice Press, 1996), pp. 111–112. Used by permission.

NOTES

3

God? Are You Fair?

Session Focus: How does our experience of evil, pain, and suffering in the world relate to the way we perceive God? If God is in control, why are things such a mess? How do we experience God's love and God's justice?

Scriptures Used: Job (excerpts); Ecclesiastes 3:1–8; Luke 13:1–5; John 9:1–7; Romans 8:18–28, 31–39

BEFORE THE SESSION

As a child, I would occasionally run to my father, complaining of some injustice imparted to me, usually at the hands of one of my siblings. As I bemoaned the fact that "it isn't fair," my father would often reply, "Life isn't fair."

Maturity has convinced me that my father was right, in many areas, but especially this one. Life isn't always fair. Consider events from recent years. A bomb explodes in front of a building in Oklahoma City. One hundred sixty-eight people are killed, including innocent children playing in a day-care center. A beloved princess dies in a tragic auto accident in Paris, France, just as she is becoming known for the charitable causes she championed. Siamese twins are born joined at the abdomen, sharing a single pair of legs and most internal organs. At some point a decision may have to be made to sacrifice one child so that the other can live. A tornado strikes a church building on Sunday morning, killing many people who were gathered to worship. A disturbed child gets a gun and opens fire on classmates and teachers at school.

These examples not only prove the saying that life isn't fair but also raise questions about God. Is God fair? Where is God in these tragedies? If God is all-powerful and all-loving, how could God allow innocent people to die? Why do bad things happen to good people? And why do good things happen to bad people? Predatory people can amass fortunes through unethical business practices and live long, healthy, luxurious lives.

The question of evil is one that has troubled religious people since the beginning of time. Some point to the story of the Garden of Eden as the beginning of evil (this story can be found in Genesis 3). They insist that when humankind first sinned against God, they allowed evil to enter the world, and it has been prospering ever since. Others can reconcile evil caused by humans as the result of human sinfulness but struggle with natural evil—that is, tragedies caused by non-human actions, tornadoes, floods, earthquakes, and so on.

Still, the question of God's role in evil remains. Is God an active participant with some hidden plan (implied in the well-meaning phrase, "It must be God's will"), or is God an unwilling spectator, unable to stop evil from occurring? Or is there another explanation? This session explores these questions and some of the answers proposed by scripture and theologians. What do you think? Is life fair? Where is God when evil occurs?

1. Tell about your own experiences

What situations cause you to wonder if life is fair? Think of an instance, in your own life or in the world at large, of a time when life seemed particularly unfair. Was it a natural disaster? The death of a loved one or an innocent? Perhaps it was something

as simple as a person getting away with a particularly evil act, or an innocent person being wrongfully punished. Tell your story to the group. Listen to the stories told by others. Don't attempt to analyze, rationalize, or theorize, just listen and affirm others for their willingness to tell their stories.

Invite group members to tell their stories. If the group is large, separate into smaller groups. Listen nonjudgmentally and with empathy. Be aware that some may tell particularly personal and painful stories.

2. Pray together

Pray briefly together. Use the following prayer or one of your own.

Creator and Creating God, we don't always understand why things are the way they are. We come to you with questions unanswered, wrestling for insights and knowledge. Open our eyes and our ears in this session. Help us to listen to one another and to you. Bless us as we struggle with the tough questions of our faith. Bless us as we struggle to grow closer to you. To you be the power and the glory always. Amen.

CONNECTING WITH THE THEME

Read and discuss. You may want to bring other definitions to consider.

3. Define evil

What is evil? Is evil a person or a force that exists in society? Are people evil? Or is it just that people get caught up in bad situations? For the purpose of this discussion, *evil is that which causes separation from God and causes harm to others.* In regard to human activity, evil is a rebellion against God. However, natural forces can also be experienced as evil in that they can cause destruction and suffering. How does this definition fit with your understanding of evil? What is God's role in the process? If God created all things, did God create evil, as well?

4. Meet Job

In the Bible, the book of Job tells the story of a man severely tested by God. Originally prosperous, he loses everything that is near and dear to him: his fortune, his family, even his health. His neighbors gather to offer their interpretation of why this evil has befallen him.

Rather than accept their answers, Job begs God to explain. At the end of the book, God speaks to Job in a whirlwind, offering an explanation that is hard to interpret, and for many, hard to accept.

The name *Job* may mean "Where is the divine father?" or "hated/persecuted one." Either interpretation seems fitting for the story. Its authorship is uncertain, as is the date it was written. It was probably written some time between the seventh and fourth centuries before Christ (B.C.), although parts of it may have circulated as an oral story much earlier. It possibly came into its present form during the Babylonian exile. This was a time after the Babylonian armies had destroyed Jerusalem and its temple and carried all but the poorest Israelites into captivity in Babylon, sometime after 586 B.C. If so, it is likely an attempt to explain undeserved suffering to a people who were struggling with the question of why bad things were happening and where God was in the destruction.

Read and discuss especially the opening, chapters 1—2; the response of friends, chapters 4, 8, 11; Job's response, chapter 23; and God's response, Job 38; 41:1–11. Parts may be assigned to small groups or individuals and reported back to the whole.

Browse through the book of Job. How is suffering explained in the opening chapters? Is this meant to be an explanation for all suffering, or merely a device to set up Job's particular situation? How do Job's friends respond? How does Job respond? Finally, how does God respond? After browsing through the book as a whole, consider the following questions: Does this book offer an acceptable explanation for the presence of evil? Why or why not? What image of God is portrayed? Do you agree with Job? his friends? the explanation given by God? What further questions does this book raise in regard to evil and suffering?

5. Review the scriptures

Read and discuss. Briefly consider these scripture passages: Ecclesiastes 3:1–8; Romans 8:18–28; Luke 13:1–5; John 9:1–7.

Other scripture passages offer other explanations for why bad things happen. Consider some of these scriptures. What explanations are offered? How do they fit with your understanding of God?

6. Define the problem

Read and discuss.

In its simplest form, the problem of evil exists because of three assertions that are difficult to reconcile. First, God is all-powerful. Second, God is all-loving. Third, evil exists. (Bad things happen to good people.) If God is all-loving and all-powerful, how can God allow good people to suffer? How do you reconcile these three statements?

7. Ponder explanations

As the size of the group allows, divide the following explanations of evil among four teams or individuals. Each team or individual can present one of the explanations in a mock debate. Discuss which explanation makes the most sense and why.

As seen in the earlier activities, scripture and theology offer several explanations for the presence of evil. Over the course of human history, many other explanations have been offered. Several are briefly described here. Which make sense to you? Why? What are the strengths of each argument? What are the weaknesses? What other explanations have you heard? After hearing these four, do other possible explanations come to mind?

A. The Devil Made Me Do It. Some explain the presence of evil by pointing to a supernatural being who is responsible, one who is in conflict with God. Various names have been given to this being: Satan, the Devil, Evil Personified. One attractive part of this explanation is that evil seems to be more than the sum of its parts, that an active force of evil greater than humankind is necessary to account for a world of genocide and conflict. Yet perhaps that's the easy way out. The result is the same: Someone else is responsible. This explanation accounts for the presence of evil while absolving God of the blame. Unfortunately, it also absolves humankind of responsibility. Those who commit horrendous acts are in the hands of an evil power. The perpetrator then becomes as much a victim as the victims themselves.

B. It's for Your Own Good. This explanation really has two parts. First, it explains the occurrence of bad things as a part of God's infinite plan. This is implied in statements such as "It's God's will," or "Someday we'll understand why this happened." It resolves the dilemma of how evil can exist in the hands of an all-powerful, all-loving God by, in effect, denying that evil exists. Things may seem to be bad, but if we could only see things as God sees them, we would understand that they are working for a greater good. Many find this a very comforting idea. At least it offers some kind of explanation for the tragedies we experience. Others, though, find it very troubling. If God is all-loving and all-powerful, cannot God find another way to accomplish this hidden purpose without allowing innocent people to suffer?

The second part of this explanation is that sometimes suffering is caused by human actions, and God allows us to suffer the consequences of our actions. For instance, studies have shown that smokers have a much higher risk of contracting lung cancer and other fatal diseases. If one then suffers cancer, is it fair to say that God caused it? Or did God simply allow the individual to suffer the consequences of his or her actions? This explanation makes sense on some level, but still fails to explain why some innocent people may suffer (a child that suffers asthma from secondhand smoke, for instance).

C. I Can't Help It. A third explanation is that God simply can not stop some evil from occurring. In creation, humans were given free will, the ability to choose between good and evil. Sometimes, we humans choose evil. So, though God is all-powerful and all-loving, evil exists because humans sometimes choose wrongly. This human sin can be individual, such as a single gunman storming into a schoolyard and randomly firing at students, or it can be systemic evil, rooted in the political, economic, and social systems. An example of this is the polluting of our planet, resulting in increased disease and decreased resources. Some sins we bring on ourselves, out of

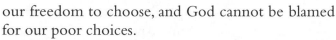

our freedom to choose, and God cannot be blamed for our poor choices.

While this accounts for human evil, it still leaves the question of natural disasters. Do hurricanes, earthquakes, and the like have the power to choose good over evil? Some argue yes, at least in a limited sense. Many of the same forces that cause a gentle breeze to bring refreshment on a hot day can also cause a deadly tornado to descend on a populated area. While natural events don't have the same consciousness or capacity to choose good over evil as humans do, the same basic forces can cause either growth or destruction. Because of this freedom to choose, God is not responsible for evil. Yet this still leaves the question, If God is all-powerful, why does God allow evil? Why doesn't God simply stop it from occurring?

D. Stuff Happens. A fourth explanation is simply that bad things sometimes happen. Sometimes it is the result of human sin and only humans are to blame. Sometimes, though, it just happens, for no good reason, or just from dumb luck. Sometimes people get cancer, not through any fault of their own, but just because. Sometimes people are injured or killed simply because they had the misfortune to be in the wrong place at the right time. There isn't a good explanation. It just is.

This explanation still doesn't answer the question of why God doesn't stop the bad things, but that isn't its purpose. Instead it attempts to accept that bad things do happen and looks for ways that God can bring something good out of it. For instance, the death of Princess Diana in 1997 was undoubtedly a tragedy. The investigation has provided several reasons for the accident, including the fact that the driver was under the influence of alcohol, and the passengers, with one exception, were not wearing seat belts. It was a terrible accident. But can God bring anything good out of it? Indeed, the outpouring of grief following Diana's death caused many to reevaluate the consequences of drinking and driving and failing to wear seat belts. Even more, the memorial fund set up in the name of Princess Diana has continued the work she began and raised millions of dollars for worthy causes. One can rightly ask if such results were worth her death—of course not. But God was able to take a senseless tragedy and bring some good out of it, a resurrection of sorts. How does this explanation fit with your experience of evil and suffering? What other examples can you think of in which God was able to take something bad and make out of it something good?

8. Explore ways to overcome evil with good

Read and discuss.

If we accept the notion that evil exists and that part of our role as Christians is to try to overcome evil in our world, how can we go about it? Look back over the examples of suffering in "Before the Session." What are things we (meaning the human race) might have done to prevent such tragedies? What might we be doing after the tragedy to help those in need? How might God overcome evil with good? How can we help?

Think about events in the headlines today. What evil is currently capturing national, local, or your own personal attention? What can you be doing about it? In what ways is your congregation working to bring good out of evil or to prevent evil from occurring?

9. Find hope in the midst of pain

Read and discuss.

Discuss ways that God is present in the midst of suffering.

Regardless of your understanding of why evil exists, our understanding of a God of love requires that God must in some way be working through, or perhaps in spite of, the suffering that exists. Read Romans 8:31–39. What hope does it offer for those who are suffering? When were times (if any) in your own experience when God seemed especially close even though times were hard?

Dr. Martin Luther King, Jr., knew what it meant to suffer, and he saw firsthand the damage evil could do. In his sermon "Our God is Able," he recounts the moment when God's presence in the midst of suffering became especially real. It was the middle of the night, shortly after the Montgomery, Alabama, bus protest, when an anonymous caller telephoned the King home. The voice on the phone was ominous, threatening Dr. King's life and that of his family. Unable to sleep, Dr. King began pacing in his kitchen, finally falling before God at the kitchen table. In the middle of the night, Dr. King begged for God's strength and wisdom. He writes, "At that moment I experienced the presence of the Divine as I had never before experienced him. It seemed as though I could hear the quiet assurance of an inner voice, saying, "Stand up for righteousness, stand up for truth. God will be at your side forever."

King goes on to say that three nights later a bomb did explode in front of his home. Fortunately, no one was injured. Still, he says, he could accept the news of the bombing calmly. He writes, "I knew now that God is able to give us the interior resources to face the storms and problems of life."[1]

How do you understand Dr. King's experience of God's presence? In light of how his life ended, what might he have meant by the title of his sermon, "Our God is Able"?

10. Write a letter to God

Write a letter to God. What questions do you need to ask about the presence of evil in our world? If you choose, read the letter aloud, or commit it to God silently in your heart.

11. Listen for God's answer

Spend several minutes reflecting silently on the letters to God. In quiet meditation, listen for God's answers. In what ways does God offer you reassurance of God's continuing presence?

Close the session with a brief group prayer.

[1]Martin Luther King, Jr., *Strength to Love* (Philadelphia: Fortress Press, 1963), pp. 113–114.

How Does Jesus Fit In?

Session Focus: Who is Jesus? Why does the Christian community believe that Jesus is the Messiah? How could Jesus be both human and God?

Scriptures Used: Matthew 1:23; 11:2–3; 12:23; 16:13–20; 27:11, 37, 54; Mark 1:11; Luke 6:5; 22:39–42; John 1:1, 38; 6:15; 11:35; 19:28; 20:31; 21:9–14; Ephesians 2:20; Philippians 2:5–11; Colossians 1:15–20; Hebrews 12:2.

BEFORE THE SESSION

Since the moment the adult Jesus appeared on the scene sometime around A.D. 30, people have been struggling to make sense of his life, death, and resurrection. According to the Gospels, people were questioning his significance even while he was still engaged in his earthly ministry. When John the Baptist was in prison, he sent messengers to Jesus asking, "Are you the one who is to come, or are we to wait for another?" (Matthew 11:3f.) Jesus asked his disciples, "Who do people say that the Son of Man is?" and they responded with numerous answers, "John the Baptist...Elijah...Jeremiah or one of the prophets." Jesus then asked, "But who do you say that I am?" (Matthew 16:15f) On trial before Pilate, Jesus was asked, "Are you the King of the

Jews?" (Matthew 27:11). And upon the cross, as Jesus died, a Roman soldier proclaimed, "Truly this man was the God's Son!" (Matthew 27:54).

One might think that after his death and resurrection, the question of Jesus' identity would have been settled, but it wasn't. The early church struggled to define who Jesus was, and how to make sense of his humanity and divinity. Peter and other disciples of Jesus proclaimed the crucified and risen Christ as the fulfillment of Jewish prophecy. Soon the movement was drawing in converts from beyond Judaism, who brought their own questions and understandings from the world of Greek philosophy and other religions. Paul, a new Jewish convert, began spreading churches around the Near East and into Europe, and helped to redefine Jesus as the one who broke down the barriers between Jews and Gentiles (non-Jews), and the one whose death broke down the barriers between humanity and God (Ephesians 1—3). Over the first few decades of the Christian movement, the stories of Jesus were transmitted through the preaching and teachings of apostles and other leaders, many of whom had known Jesus personally. As they began to die away (or were killed in times of persecution), others wrote the stories down so they would not be lost. Still others, during the last three decades of the first century A.D., reworked the stories into gospels, written that people "may come to believe that Jesus is the Messiah, the Son of God" (John 20:31).

In later centuries, the churches continued to struggle with the question of how Jesus could be both human and divine. Different teachers and movements offered alternate solutions, generally lifting up one part of Jesus' nature at the expense of others. The church gathered its leaders and teachers to develop creeds to help express its belief that Jesus Christ was fully human, with all the frailties and suffering involved, and fully divine, the Word of God, intimately a part of God. The church had finally, officially, stated its understanding and has been struggling to make sense of that understanding ever since.

In recent years, Jesus' identity and significance have again been a source of struggle. The quest for the historical Jesus has led many scholars to attempt to uncover exactly what Jesus said and did in his earthly ministry. They believe that if we could separate Jesus' true actions from those attributed to him later, we would have a better understanding of who Jesus was. Others question the criteria of these scholars, the standards by which they decide what parts of the gospel records are historical and which are not. Still others have focused on the events of the resurrection. Was it a bodily resurrection? Or was it a spiritual resurrection? Does it matter? The Shroud of Turin, traditionally believed to be the burial cloth of Jesus, was disproved several years back through the modern technique of carbon dating. Even so, its supporters are citing new evidence that the modern testing failed and that we do indeed have proof of Jesus' resurrection. Does it matter? Does it make a difference to our faith if the shroud is, or is not, the actual burial cloth of Jesus?

Perhaps we will never fully resolve all of the questions surrounding the life, death, and resurrection of Jesus of Nazareth, the one Christians affirm as the Son of God. But perhaps we can answer the most important one, the one Jesus himself asked, "Who do you say that I am?"

Mini Glossary

Messiah—a Hebrew term meaning "anointed one," originally applied to kings and priests but later to describe one that God would send to usher in God's reign.

A.D.—*Anno Domini,* Latin for "the Year of our Lord," dated from the birth of Christ, as reckoned by medieval scholars. Their reckoning was off, since Jesus was probably born between 4 and 7 B.C. (Before Christ).

Gospels—Accounts of the life, death, and resurrection of Christ. The root word means "good news." The Gospels according to Matthew, Mark, Luke, and John make up the first four books of the New Testament.

John the Baptist—a prophet who proclaimed the coming reign of God and called people to repent of (turn away from) their sins and be baptized. He baptized Jesus.

CONNECTING WITH ONE ANOTHER

Open the session with a few moments of catching up with one another's lives. Encourage members to talk about events of the past week, struggles as well as joys. Take a few moments to pray together, asking for God's guidance and support. Then move into Activity 1, inviting responses to its questions.

CONNECTING WITH THE THEME

1. Respond to a call 🔑

Early in his ministry, Jesus began preaching good news about God's purposes and healed some people who were sick. Then he called some people to be his followers and to learn from him. We don't know how many said, "What? No way!" But a few responded, left their occupations and families, and began to travel with him from town to town.

Imagine that you are living in Galilee nearly twenty centuries ago. You have heard stories about a carpenter's son who is causing some excitement. You may even have listened to him teach. Then, as you are at work one day, he looks you in the eye and says, "Come, follow me." Remember that, at this point, he isn't asking you to accept him as the Messiah, but just to come and learn from him.

How would you make your decision? What information would you need to make that decision? What questions might you ask of Jesus? What factors might make you decline the invitation? What factors might make you accept it?

2. Begin writing a gospel 🔑

Imagine that your group has been transported to a lunar colony. You want to start a Christian community there, but nobody brought a Bible! It will be a year before a supply rocket will arrive. In the meantime, you have decided to create a makeshift gospel of your own, to help recall the essential stories about Jesus. Today you want to begin work on writing the gospel. Below is a series of "hangers" or categories to use in outlining it. Recall together stories and connect them to a category. (Don't worry about telling the story in detail—you are outlining and summarizing, not re-creating.)

▲ Birth

▲ Beginning of ministry

▲ Miracles and healings

▲ Teachings and parables

▲ Suffering, death, and resurrection

3. Retell a story or teaching

After the group has outlined its gospel and listed the stories that it should include, work together in teams to tell one of the stories or teachings in your own words. Once your team has completed its work, present the story or teaching to the rest of the group. You now have written a part of your gospel for the moon. How big a challenge would it be to create an entire gospel this way?

4. Ask questions about Jesus

Anyone who has an interest in Christianity has questions about Jesus. Some are significant, others less so. Some are answerable, others are not. Perhaps some questions grew out of trying to create a new gospel; others may have been at the back of your mind since childhood.

Now is the time to ask, and to listen to your friend's questions. Even if you know how to answer someone else's question, don't. Get all the questions out first.

As time allows, go back to some of the questions and discuss them. Perhaps someone in the group can offer answers, or at least responses. Use Bible study tools to help research some of the questions. Or adopt a question—yours or someone else's—by taking it home and reflecting upon it or researching it. Then come back and discuss it during the next session.

5. Answer Jesus' question

Read Matthew 16:13–20. In this passage Jesus asks his disciples to identify him. Not only does he want to know what others are saying about him, but he wants to know what those closest to him think. Discuss within the group your answer to Jesus' question. Who do you say Jesus is? Think also about what others say about him. What does your church say? What does the pastor say? What does the world in general say? What images of Jesus do you affirm? Which images do you reject? Who is Jesus to you?

6. Name Jesus in scripture

Read scriptures as a group, or divide into teams and assign a passage to each team. Some passages to consider are: Matthew 1:23; Matthew 12:23; Mark 1:11; Luke 6:5; John 1:38; Ephesians 2:20; Hebrews 12:2.

Scripture offers many names for Jesus. Explore some of the scripture passages. What names are used for Jesus? How do these names expand or enhance your understanding of Jesus? List the names or titles for Jesus on paper, newsprint, or chalkboard. Which have special meaning for you? Which raise questions? What other names have you heard or known?

7. Find Jesus in early Christian hymns

Even before the Gospels were written, Christians worshiped, told stories, and sang hymns about Jesus. Some of the earliest Christian hymns are preserved, at least in part, in two of Paul's letters. Read Philippians 2:5–11 and Colossians 1:15–20. What images of Jesus are portrayed in these hymns? How did the hymn writers understand Jesus' divinity?

8. Understand Jesus as Messiah

Read and discuss.

Christians today often speak of Jesus as the

Messiah. So often have these two names been connected that they have, for Christians at least, become synonymous. The Messiah is Jesus and Jesus is the Messiah. (*Christ* is the Greek word for messiah—both mean one who is anointed.)

But such was not the case during Jesus' lifetime. The Jewish people were expecting a messiah. Indeed, they had been keeping watch for generations. Under political oppression from the Romans, their expectations were exceptionally high. Yet Judaism existed in many branches, and they had different understandings of what *messiah* would mean, and what the messiah would do and be. For some, the messiah would be a king who would continue the royal lineage of David. The messiah, though divinely appointed, would be a human endowed with special gifts of wisdom and righteousness. The messiah would bring peace to Israel and restore God's people to power. For others, the messiah would be a political leader who would lead them away from foreign domination and back to wholeness and independence. For others, the messiah would usher in the end of a sinful age and bring in a time of conflict when all the powers of the world would eventually be overturned, and God would reign over the whole earth.

Some scripture passages seem to point to this understanding of messiah in relation to Jesus. After he fed the multitudes, according to John 6:15, the people attempted to make Jesus a "king." On the cross, above his head, was a sign proclaiming Jesus "King of the Jews" (Matthew 27:37).

Christians do not see Jesus as a military leader, but as a spiritual leader. The triumph over oppressive powers was not a victory over a foreign government, but over the powers of sin and death. Jesus' kingship was not over a geographical area, but over the hearts of believers. Christians proclaim that Jesus is Savior and Lord, the Messiah, because through him, we have been given wholeness and life.

How do you understand *messiah*? What meaning does the term have for us today?

9. Struggle with Jesus' divinity

In Colossians 1:17, Christ is "before all things, and in him all things hold together." The Gospel of John says that Jesus is the Word (Logos), and that "In the beginning was the Word, and the Word was with God, and the Word was God" (John 1:1). Clearly, New Testament writers believed Jesus to be divine. It is not always clear whether Jesus was God, or with God, or both. Yet, the scriptures also portray Jesus as human. In the garden before his crucifixion, Jesus prayed that God might take away this cup of suffering (Luke 22:39–42). When his good friend Lazarus died, Jesus wept. He grieved like any of us would (John 11:35). On the cross, Jesus cried out for drink, saying he was thirsty (John 19:28). And after the resurrection, Jesus shared a breakfast of grilled fish with his disciples, thus proving to them he was a real physical being and not merely a ghost (John 21:9–14). How can this be? How can Jesus be both God and human at the same time? If Jesus always existed with God, what does it mean to say Jesus was born of Mary in Bethlehem? Did Jesus have to die? How do you make sense of Jesus' divinity? How do you reconcile the Jesus of history with the Son of God of our faith? What are the implications of saying Jesus was only human? only divine? How is it important to affirm both?

10. Make a banner

Have supplies available if the group wishes to make a banner.

If you made a banner to glorify God during Session 2, consider making another one using a symbol, an image, or words about Jesus as the Christ. How will he be pictured? Will you use symbols from his earthly ministry? his resurrected presence? or both? How can you create an image of Jesus that reflects both his humanity and his divinity?

Make one banner as a group or smaller ones as teams.

11. Live as a Christian

CONNECTING WITH LIFE

Read and discuss.

Tradition tells us that the followers of Jesus were first called "Christians" in Antioch of Syria. The term is used only three times in the New Testament. It may originally have been a derogatory term given by non-Christians but quickly came to be accepted by those who believed that Jesus of Nazareth was the Christ. The word *Christian* means one who follows or is a servant of Christ. How are we called to be servants of Christ? In what ways can we be examples of Christ to others?

12. Become Christ's hands

Reputedly there is a church in San Diego, California, that has a statue of Jesus Christ near the front entrance. The statue shows Jesus with arms outstretched, but at the end of the arms there are no hands. The statue was created that way intentionally to give a message. Jesus Christ has no hands but ours. If his work is to be accomplished, our hands, and hearts, and minds, will have to do it. A popular question has resurfaced in recent years: What would Jesus do? What are we called to do, if we are to be Jesus' followers?

Make a list of the ways that your church is doing, and might be able to do, Christ's work in the world. Make a commitment, as individuals and as a group, to be Christ's hands in the week to come. Select a project, either ongoing or a single event, that will be a living example of Christ's hands at work. How might our efforts make Jesus more real to others?

CONNECTING WITH GOD

13. Sing a hymn

Sing or say together a hymn that praises Jesus.

Consider supplying hymnals.

Look in your church's hymnal for ideas. Some suggestions might be "All Hail the Power of Jesus' Name!" "O, How I Love Jesus," "Jesus, Thou Joy of Loving Hearts," or "Fairest Lord Jesus." Be especially mindful of the images of Jesus portrayed in the hymns.

14. Give thanks to God

Close the session with a brief prayer such as the one below or your own.

Almighty and most gracious God,

We praise you for the gift of your Son, Jesus Christ. He entered our world in the most humble of ways and faced death in the most painful of ways. Yet, it was through him that we came to know you. Forgive us the times we have failed to recognize Christ's presence in our lives. Forgive us the times we, too, would have despised him, rejected him, or ignored him. Forgive us when we have failed to be the hands of Christ to others. Renew our spirits and rekindle our hearts, that we may proclaim Christ's presence in the world and rejoice in his presence in our lives. In your Son's name we pray. Amen.

5

Is the Spirit a Who?

Session Focus: We have many different images of the work of the Holy Spirit from the Bible, theology, and our own experiences. Yet an understanding of the Spirit remains as elusive as the Spirit itself. What is the connection between God's Spirit and creation? the church? our spiritual lives?

Scriptures Used: Genesis 1:2; Psalm 104:30; Isaiah 11:2; Ezekiel 2:1–2; 11:19; Mark 1:9–12; John 14:15–17, 25–31; Acts 2:1–12; 10:44–48; Romans 8:26–27.

BEFORE THE SESSION

A young minister questions her call and commitment to the church. At just the right moment, the phone rings with words of encouragement. Is this the work of the Holy Spirit?

A television evangelist lays hands on a member of the audience. The person falls back, shaking and stunned, and shouts praises to God. Is this the work of the Holy Spirit?

A church faces a financial crisis and is unable to meet payroll, bills, or outreach giving. Out of the blue, a check arrives from a former member, for just the right amount. Is this the work of the Holy Spirit?

A composer is struggling over a musical setting for the Lord's Prayer as part of a larger musical mass. Nothing seems to fit. One night the composer is dreaming, and the tune comes to him in a dream. The next morning the musician writes the score in a frenzy of creative activity. Is this the work of the Holy Spirit?

Two groups in a congregation have a bitter argument, and one family becomes inactive as a result. Years later, at a spiritual retreat, one of the active members of the church is still struggling with his feelings about the conflict. He leaves the retreat and goes to call on the alienated family, hoping to achieve some reconciliation. Is this the work of the Holy Spirit?

We can't describe God's Spirit in visual terms. Instead, we find ourselves describing not what the Spirit is, but what the Spirit does. Like a teacher describing the wind to a group of children. "But what does it look like?" they ask, to which the teacher replies, "It doesn't look like anything. We know it only from what it does. It makes the trees blow and the leaves fall. It brings a cool touch on a hot day. It can be gentle and slow, or strong and fierce. It can't be seen, but it leaves its mark on everything it touches."

The same is true of the Holy Spirit. We may not be able to see it, or even describe it apart from what it does, but its presence can be felt, and it leaves its impact wherever it goes.

What is the Spirit? Or who is the Spirit? Perhaps more importantly, the question is, "How do we recognize it when we encounter it?"

1. Tell about experiences of community

To be in community is to be together with others in a group and to feel a sense of unity and belonging within that group. Think of a time you felt in community with others. It might have been in a family group around a holiday table; it might have been in a small group like this one; it might have been at worship; it might have been at a rock concert; or it might have been at a political rally. The settings for community vary widely. But what created the experience of community that you recalled? How

CONNECTING WITH ONE ANOTHER

Spend a few moments reconnecting as a group. Encourage people to tell about special problems or concerns or joys. Pray briefly together, asking for God's presence in your midst. Then invite the group members to tell about their experiences in community.

long-lasting was it? What influence did it have on your life?

2. Pool information about the Holy Spirit

What do you think of when you hear the term *Holy Spirit* (or the older translation, *Holy Ghost*)? In what contexts have you heard (or read) the term? Different Christian faith traditions emphasize the Spirit in different ways, so you may hear a wide variety of responses. Be sure to ask questions that you may have about the Holy Spirit. They may not all be answered in this session, but they could offer a starting point into more reading or research on the subject.

3. Imagine the Holy Spirit in scripture

The Holy Spirit is most often described in terms of what it does. Occasionally, though, it is given a "face," so to speak. The writers use imagery to help us grasp the nature of the Spirit. Browse through several scripture passages. What images are used for the Holy Spirit? What kind of pictures do they paint? Consider such passages as Psalm 104:30; Ezekiel 2:1–2; Mark 1:9–12; John 14:25–31; Acts 2:1–4.

4. Understand the Spirit in the original biblical languages

In the original languages of the Bible, the same words were used for "wind," "breath," and "spirit." The latter term was used with animals and people as well as with God. God's spirit "breathed" life into creation.

The Old Testament was written in Hebrew. The Hebrew word for spirit, *ruach* (ROO-awk) refers primarily to God's Spirit in three ways. First, the Holy Spirit participates in creation. Genesis 1:2, for example, says that the Spirit or Wind of God was

Ask someone in the group to list on paper the questions that are raised.

If the group is large, divide into teams. Make a list of images on paper, newsprint, or chalkboard.

Read and discuss.

moving over the face of the waters. Second, the Holy Spirit is the source of inspiration and power for those whom God chooses. The Holy Spirit gave insight to Moses and the prophets, as well as to the kings and judges. The prophet Isaiah, for example, talks about one that God would send (interpreted by some to be Jesus) who would receive the Spirit and its gifts. Isaiah 11:2 says, "The Spirit of the LORD shall rest on him, the spirit of wisdom and understanding, the spirit of counsel and might, the spirit of knowledge and fear of the LORD." The third use of the term is found in the Holy Spirit's presence with God's chosen people. In Ezekiel 11:19, God promises to give God's people "one heart, and put a new spirit within them."

The Greek word for Spirit, used in the New Testament, is *pneuma* (NEW-ma). The same understandings of Spirit are present as in the Old Testament, but a new understanding is introduced. Because of the close relationship between Jesus and God, the Spirit is also used in connection with Jesus. Thus the Holy Spirit represents not only the continuing activity of God but also the continuing presence of Christ. We can see this especially clearly in John 14 when Jesus describes the Spirit as Counselor, and promises that even after his death, the disciples will not be left alone.

How do these understandings of Spirit continue today? How do we see the Spirit working as a participant in creation? as a source of divine inspiration? as a gift to the community of believers? as the continuing presence of Christ? How and in what ways are these aspects of the Spirit made known?

Harper's Bible Dictionary defines the Holy Spirit as "the mysterious power or presence of God in nature or with individuals and communities, inspiring or empowering them with qualities they would not otherwise possess."[1] What is your response to this definition? What examples can you think of where the Spirit "inspires" or "empowers" communities or individuals?

5. Experience the Spirit in song

If this hymn is in your hymnal and/or is known to the group, sing it together and then discuss it. If not, read it in unison.

Many hymns describe the work of the Spirit. One of the most familiar is "Spirit of God, Descend upon My Heart," written in the 1860s by George Croly and Frederick C. Atkinson. Sing or say the words of the hymn together. Then form teams to summarize each verse. How does it describe the work of the Spirit? What images does it use? How do we experience the presence of the Spirit? You may want to illustrate the verses through drawings, creative movement, or other forms of art.

Spirit of God, Descend upon My Heart

Spirit of God, descend upon my heart;
wean it from earth, through all its pulses move;
stoop to my weakness, mighty as thou art,
and make me love thee as I ought to love.

I ask no dream, no prophet ecstasies,
no sudden rending of the veil of clay,
no angel visitant, no opening skies,
but take the dimness of my soul away.

Teach me to feel that thou art always nigh;
teach me the struggles of the soul to bear:
to check the rising doubt, the rebel sigh;
teach me the patience of unanswered prayer.

Teach me to love thee as thine angels love,
one holy passion filling all my frame;
the baptism of the heaven descended Dove.
My heart an altar, and thy love the flame.

As time allows, look for other songs about the Holy Spirit in the hymnal. Read aloud the words to verses that have special meaning.

6. Place the Spirit within life's experience

At what point does the Holy Spirit enter into the life of the believer? Is it after baptism, or before? Is it a gift bestowed after making a commitment to God, or is it the power that draws us to God in the first place? The scriptures send mixed messages on this point. In some instances, the gift of the Holy Spirit seems to come upon believers after baptism and after they make their commitments to God. Such would seem to be the case in the story of the first Pentecost in Acts 2:1–12. Here the community as a whole, led by the disciples, receives the rushing wind of the Holy Spirit. However, scripture also tells us that at times baptism follows the gift of the Holy Spirit. In Acts 10:44–48, the apostle Peter found himself preaching to a crowd of Gentiles. The gift of the Holy Spirit fell upon them. Peter then called for water to baptize the crowd, saying, "Can anyone withhold the water for baptizing these people who have received the Holy Spirit just as we have?"

It's possible, of course, that both can be true. The Holy Spirit can be God's gentle leading as it nudges us toward belief. It can also be the fresh anointing of God's presence that follows our confession and baptism into Christ's church. In fact, it would have to be true that the Holy Spirit was ours all along, for it comes to us not as a result of something we do, but as a gracious gift of God. Some would say that God's Spirit reaches out to us all, but that we may or may not discern its presence. What do you think? At what point does the Spirit enter into the life of the believer? At what point—if any—were you first aware of the presence of the Spirit in your life?

7. Discern the Spirit's presence

Look back over the situations described in "Before the Session." Are they the work of the Spirit? How can you tell? By what criteria do we

Is the Spirit a Who?

judge whether it is the Spirit at work or merely coincidence? Or are we able to judge at all?

One way to discern the Spirit's presence is to measure it against the images of Spirit in scripture. Does this seem to be a way God would work? Does this seem consistent with the gracious God we know through scripture? Does this fit with the definition given above for the Holy Spirit? Some questions can be answered only with hindsight. Did this activity or gift of the Spirit draw the believer closer to God or open up new relationships with God?

Even as we are measuring the experience against scripture, we are also called to use our reason, experience, and the tradition of the church to discern the Holy Spirit's activity. Does this experience make sense? Does it fit with experiences we know? Is it consistent with the ways the Spirit has been at work over the past 2,000 years? Certainly God could choose to work in a new way if God chose. Still, using past experience as a guide is a helpful means of recognizing the Spirit in the present.

Finally, is it important to analyze whether or not an experience is the work of the Spirit? Why or why not?

> Discuss together the examples given in "Before the Session," as well as other experiences from the group members' lives. Use the questions and tools above to attempt to discern the Spirit.

8. Make a banner

Complete the Trinity banner project by creating a banner celebrating the work of the Holy Spirit. Consider what images, colors and fabrics to choose that will convey the group's understanding of the Holy Spirit.

Take a few moments to reflect on the three banners together, one for each person of the Trinity—Creator, Christ, and the Holy Spirit. Many churches have a defined doctrine of the Trinity in their creeds or statements of faith. Other churches don't have such a doctrine but accept these as three ways that one God expresses Godself. What other symbols have you seen in religious art and architecture that point to the Trinity, or to each part of it?

9. Discuss personal experiences of the Spirit

This activity works best when the group contains members from several different places on the Christian journey. Not every group member should be expected to have a story.

Discuss occasions in which the Holy Spirit seemed present. The occasion may be a personal story, or it may be one with a wider context, such as an event reported through the media. In what way was the Spirit known? Was it immediately recognizable, or did it only become obvious in hindsight? Was it a personal experience, known only to one, or did many people experience the same thing? What impact did this experience have? Was it short lived or long lasting? This is a time simply for listening, discussing, and reflecting.

10. Return to the questions

Needed: list of questions from Activity 2.

Look again at the questions that the group raised near the beginning of this session. Which ones were partially answered during the session? Which ones were overlooked? Consider ways that the group members can find more information, such as an interview with a pastor or teacher of religion, reading, or a search on the Internet.

11. Reflect on the Spirit's role in prayer

CONNECTING WITH GOD

The Spirit is that part of God's nature that invites us closer to God and to one another. Romans 8:26–27 is a wonderful passage that offers grounds of hope for Christians under stress and persecution.

Review the article and call the group into silent meditation. After a few minutes of silence, invite people to talk about any observations they might have had.

In John 14:15–17, Jesus talks about the Spirit as an advocate for the disciples, one that will defend and encourage them in troubled times. Here, Paul talks about the Spirit's interceding, reconciling us to God. When we are so caught up in a situation that we can't put our own feelings into words, our very sighs become prayers through the Spirit's intervention. Often we get frustrated trying to pray, thinking of all

> ## Help from the Spirit
> Likewise the Spirit helps us in our weakness; for we do not know how to pray as we ought, but that very Spirit intercedes with sighs too deep for words. And God, who searches the heart, knows what is the mind of the Spirit, because the Spirit intercedes for the saints according to the will of God.
>
> Romans 8:26–27

the barriers between God and us. The Spirit is at work breaking down the barriers, and God hears our sighs of frustration, and God cares. Or, perhaps at the birth of a child or a glorious experience of nature, our sighs of joy become prayers.

Relax. Spend a few moments in silence. Meditate upon the Spirit of God, and how that Spirit seeks to draw you into deeper relationship with God.

12. Choose a response

The Spirit is God's creative energy at work, so spend some time being creative. Write, draw, paint, sculpt, sew, sing, play, dance, weave, mime, plant, or recite.

The Spirit brings our hearts and souls into harmony with God, so spend some more time in contemplation or meditation. Play quiet music or a recording of sounds from nature, relax, and open yourselves.

The Spirit calls us outward to love and serve others, so design a way to reach out in love. Plan a service project that you can work on at another time, such as volunteering at a food bank or soup kitchen, tutoring children, or visiting residents of a nursing home.

Either choose one of the following expressions for the whole group, or form teams to work on separate expressions of God's Spirit in our midst.

[1] *Harper's Bible Dictionary*, Paul J. Achtemeier, Gen. Ed. (San Francisco: Harper & Row, 1985), p. 401.

Faith Talk

NOTES

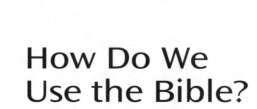

6

How Do We
Use the Bible?

Session Focus: How is—and isn't—the Bible God's Word? How do we deal with contradictions, mistakes, or teachings that seem just plain wrong? What is the basic story of the Bible? How do we interpret the Bible, and how does it interpret us?

Scriptures Used: Luke 1:1–4; John 20:30–31

BEFORE THE SESSION

Which Bible do you use? Obviously, all Christians use the Holy Bible, which, except for some variations between Protestants and Catholics, is the same throughout Christendom. There are many different versions, though. Many of us have a favorite translation, one that is most familiar and most comfortable. Some enjoy easy-to-read translations like the Good News Bible or the Contemporary English Version. Others prefer more nearly literal translations like the Revised Standard Version, New International Version, or the New Revised Standard Version. Still others place their loyalty in the old King James Version. Some prefer a paraphrase like *The Living Bible*—a paraphrase doesn't go back to the original languages in which the Bible was written but tries to tell the story in a freer way. Which Bible do you use?

People who grew up in a church often tend to prefer the version with which they were raised. It is the most familiar and its phrasing recalls to mind passages heard when they were children. Others intentionally reject the version used earlier in life in favor of one that has meaning for today, seeking new interpretations and updated language. Regardless of the translation used, it is important to remember that all of our Bibles used today are interpretations from the original texts, mostly in Hebrew or Greek. The original writings by Isaiah, Paul, Luke, or others were not written in our modern-day English, or even in the English of the 1600s, when the King James Version was first introduced.

The Bible began with the oral tradition. Stories were handed down from generation to generation by word of mouth. Only gradually did the believers feel the need to record the stories in written form. As the writings began to accumulate, the faith communities began the task of sorting and collecting the various texts. Some were given special precedence because they were considered to be most holy or sacred. The process by which the books were selected is called canonization. *Canon* referred to a measure or rule—Jewish and Christian leaders chose the books that "measured up," that had special authority. The canonization of scriptures took hundreds of years. The scriptures we know as the Old Testament or the Hebrew Bible didn't officially come together until A.D. 90. The writings to be included in the New Testament weren't officially recognized until at least A.D. 367, although most of them were recognized as Holy Scripture much earlier.

Even later came the translations from the original Hebrew and Greek to Latin, and then to other languages, a process that continues today. Today the Bible is translated into thousands of languages and dialects for people all around the world. When we look at the history of the English Bible, we discover that the first complete English New Testament was not printed until 1525, and the complete English Bible wasn't published until 1535, fifteen hundred years after Christ's death and resurrection!

Church councils, scholars, and publishers are always at work on new translations and paraphrases or new editions of older translations. Many Bibles are developed for specific groups of people. There are devotional Bibles for African Americans, for men, for women, for children, for youth, and on and on. Why do we need so many different versions? Why can't everyone use the same Bible?

One reason for the new translations is that as language changes, so does the need to make the scriptures accessible. Though the meanings behind the scriptural words are eternal, the words and phrases used to convey those meanings may change. Faithful translators make every effort to translate the words from the original language as precisely as possible while still making the passage understandable to the modern reader.

Which Bible do you use? Why? Your answer reveals as much about you as about scripture itself.

1. Play a communication game

To begin thinking about how words carry meaning, and about how we communicate with one another, play this simple game. Have one person, the artist, draw a simple picture using geometric shapes and designs. See the example at the end of this activity. The interpreter faces the audience. The artist shows the picture to the interpreter without revealing it to the audience. The interpreter then has to describe the picture in words only, without using gestures, drawings, or other forms of communication. The audience members individually then attempt to recreate the picture. When finished, compare the drawings. How close were they to the original? How many different versions did the group create?

CONNECTING WITH ONE ANOTHER

Each person needs a sheet of paper and a pen or pencil. To play, you need an artist, an interpreter, and the audience.

Discuss together the following questions. How difficult was it for the interpreter to describe the picture using only words? How difficult was it for the audience members to interpret the instructions? How can it be that everyone heard the same words, yet arrived at different understandings?

If time allows, play the game again using a different picture, only this time, have the audience work as a team to interpret the instructions. Was the result any closer to the original?

When reading the Bible, we may begin with the same words, but often Christians arrive at different understandings. Discuss how the results of the game may be similar to attempts to interpret scripture. How do our background, upbringing, and experience affect the way we read scripture? Translators often work in teams when translating scripture from one language to another. How might that help the effort to accurately convey biblical meanings in languages other than the original? How can the church as a whole work together to interpret scripture? Discuss ideas within the group.

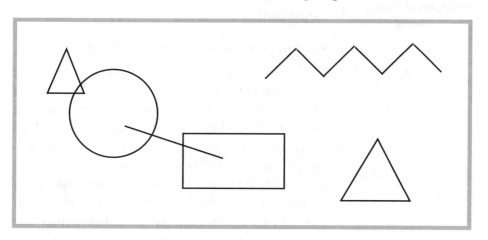

2. Pray together

After playing the game, briefly share concerns or joys from the previous week. Offer a circle prayer in which each member gives thanks for a specific event of the past week. Those who are uncomfortable praying aloud can say "pass." Close by asking God to open eyes, ears, and hearts, that scripture might be understood and lived out.

3. Understand the purpose of the Bible

The Bible was written by many people over hundreds of years, but each of the writers had a similar purpose in mind. Two of the Gospel writers spelled out their purpose in writing. Read their words and discuss together these writer's purposes. How would the purpose outlined in these two passages be similar to those of other writers? Originally many of the biblical stories were passed from generation to generation in oral form. Remembering the story of God's people was a vitally important function, but as the story was retold, it would sometimes be altered to fit new situations. Why would it become important to record the stories in written form? How might that help preserve the stories for future generations? Why would the preservation of faith stories be important?

4. Recognize various forms of biblical literature

If you were to pick up a piece of paper and read the words, "Once upon a time..." what expectations would you have for the rest of the document? What if the first words were, "Dear Sir/Madam..."? How about, "Hey Mom (Dad), Guess what?" Certain kinds of writings carry with them their own expectations. We expect a story to be different from a business letter, and a business letter to be different from a note from a loved one. Just as we encounter a variety of writing genres and writing styles in our world, so the biblical writers used various styles to convey their faith stories. Contained within the sixty-six books of the Bible are many forms of literature, including but not limited to:

▲ Hymns—songs used in worshiping God

CONNECTING WITH THE THEME

Form two teams and assign a passage to each team: Luke 1:1–4, and John 20:30–31. After each team's discussion, have the teams share with each other their passage and the results of their discussion.

Read and discuss.

Divide into teams or small groups. Allow time to discover examples of each writing style. If help is needed, some examples might include: Hymns: any of the psalms. Parables: Luke 15 and others. Letters: Romans, 1 Corinthians, and others. Historical narratives: Exodus. Heroic sagas: the story of Samson, Judges 13f. Prophetic writings: Isaiah, Jeremiah. Apocalyptic writings: Daniel, Revelation.

▲ Prayers— a believer's deepest feelings expressed to God

▲ Poetry—rhythmic, well-chosen words

▲ Parables—short stories or comparisons, often with surprise endings, that give the hearer new insight into God's ways

▲ Allegories—stories where the details point beyond themselves, to hidden or spiritual meanings

▲ Historical narratives—stories of people and events that shaped Israel or the church

▲ Prophetic sayings—messages by people who felt called to proclaim God's word to specific situations

▲ Heroic legends—good stories from the past that may not be historically true but give insight into human nature

▲ Letters—documents written to churches or individuals, offering the writer's guidance, support, judgment, and love

▲ Apocalyptic writings—literature written in times of persecution pointing toward the day of God's judgment on evil and deliverance of the faithful.

Browse through the Bible to find examples of each kind of writing. For how many categories could you find examples? How might each kind of writing have a different purpose? Why might the writer have chosen one genre over the other? How might knowing what style of literature is used help us in understanding the meaning of a passage?

5. Discuss God's role in scripture

Read and discuss.

While we can agree that the Bible is written in many different styles and in languages of long ago, Christians struggle over the question of God's role in the creation of scripture. Did God inspire the words to the point that the human writers merely recorded what God revealed? Or was scripture a human

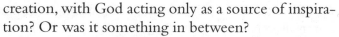

creation, with God acting only as a source of inspiration? Or was it something in between?

Faithful Christians have debated all sides of this question. In recent times, with the advent of various forms of biblical criticism, the debate has intensified. Biblical criticism brings various scholarly tools to try to understand the Bible. Biblical scholars no longer simply look at the written words; they now look at the historical context in which the words were written, the genre or form in which the text appears, and the placement of stories within the text as a whole. As scholars have become more intense in analyzing scripture in order to understand its meaning, the role of God in scripture has become an even more central question.

Some argue that scripture is inerrant—that is, without error. They believe that God's role in the creation of scripture and the formation of the Bible was so central that God actually dictated the form, meaning, and content of the text. With this understanding, any contradictions or inaccuracies within the texts are denied. God is inerrant; therefore scripture is without error.

Others argue that scripture was generated by humans. They were faithful followers of God, to be sure, but still human. Thus though God inspired them, people wrote the words. Errors, inconsistencies, even contradictions are recognized within scripture and are even to be expected. After all, the writers were only human.

A middle ground might be that God did indeed inspire scripture but not to the point of actually dictating the words. God's presence was so real and involved in the lives of the biblical writers that the texts do reflect God's inspiration, revelation, and wisdom. Contradictions may have occurred as various people responded to God's insights in different ways, and memories may have been faulty, resulting in errors of times, places, and some events. Even so, the

Faith Talk

whole of scripture is inspired, and God was active in the transmission of the living story.

What do you think? Is scripture inspired? inerrant? What role does/did God play in the formation of scripture? How do we make sense of inconsistencies within scripture?

6. Explore ways to interpret scripture

Read and discuss.

Regardless of how we understand God's role in the creation of scripture, we are still left with the task of interpreting scripture. Some argue that we simply need to read the biblical text in order to understand God's word to us. In truth, however, whenever we read about, listen to, or see an event, we interpret it through the lens of our own experience, background and upbringing. Think back to the game played at the beginning of the session. Though everyone heard the same words, people interpreted them differently. This is inevitable. Interpretation happens immediately as we attempt to make sense of the information coming to us through our senses. The question then isn't "Are we going to interpret scripture?" The question is "How are we going to interpret scripture?"

Through the ages, the church has identified three tools for interpreting scripture. They are reason, experience, and tradition. When looking at a scripture passage or scripture as a whole, we use our reason, asking, "What makes sense?" We use our experience, asking, "How have I experienced God in this way? Or how have others had a similar experience?" And we look to the tradition of the church, asking, "How has the church through the centuries understood this passage? Or how has the church understood God in this way?"

The faith community as a whole is an essential component in understanding the Bible. Where our interpretations can be limited by our own

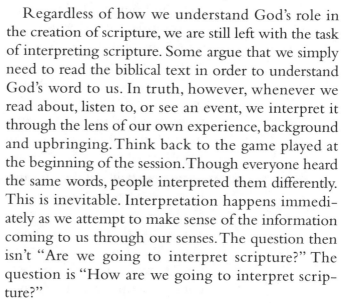

How Do We Use the Bible?

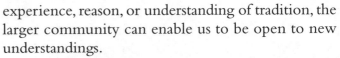

experience, reason, or understanding of tradition, the larger community can enable us to be open to new understandings.

At times, the church has erred in its interpretation of scripture. For example, for centuries the church understood scripture to be supportive of slavery, and many passages were identified and used as weapons to keep humans in bondage to one another. Reason, experience, and new traditions have worked to refine our interpretation of such passages and to reveal the deeper thread present in scripture of God's love for all humankind.

Today, other issues are being debated. One is the role of women in the church. Some passages point to women as leaders; others seem to forbid such leadership. Another "hot topic" is human sexuality, especially homosexuality. How do changed understandings of human sexuality and better understanding of biblical language change the way we interpret the Bible's teachings?

Can you think of other ways that reason, tradition, or experience have offered new interpretations of scripture? How do we use these tools in our own lives as we confront scripture, and as scripture confronts us?

7. Find the common thread in scripture

Read and discuss.

Many believe that though there are inconsistencies, repeated stories, even factual errors concerning chronology, there is a common thread that runs throughout scripture. Some see the theme as one of brokenness and healing. The Bible reveals how human sin and faulty judgment break our relationship with God and how God effects healing, both of those relationships and of humanity itself. Others see it in a similar way as the story of God's continued and continuing love for humankind. This love is so powerful that it reaches first through creation, then through the covenants with Abraham, Moses, and the Israelites, and then beyond the Jewish community to the Gentiles through the gift of God's own Son, Jesus Christ. Though humankind repeatedly rejects this gift and breaks the covenants, God continues to seek out God's people and renew relationships with them.

What do you see as the common thread in scripture? How can this common thread be used to unravel difficult passages?

CONNECTING WITH GOD

To close this session, and as a summary wrap-up of the previous sessions, allow time to discuss favorite scriptures, either within small groups or within the group as a whole. Invite each person to share a favorite passage or Bible story. Allow reluctant participants the opportunity to pass or wait until others have participated.

8. Name favorite scripture passages

What is your favorite Bible passage or story? Discuss it within the group. When did you first hear it? What meaning does it hold for you? Why is it important? How does it influence your understanding of God, Jesus, the Holy Spirit, or your purpose as a child of God?

9. Close with prayer

Pray together the following prayer, or create one of your own.

O Writer of Words and Giver of Wisdom,

For your servants who have gone before and written for us the stories of your unending love, for the heroes and heroines who risked their very lives to live out your truth and whose stories are recorded in Holy Scripture, for the witness of your faithfulness contained within the pages of our Bible, we give you glory and praise. We celebrate with you, and we give thanks for the multitude of people whose lives have been forever changed by the good news.

Make us living witnesses to this good news. Help us not only to share the biblical stories but also to live our lives as ongoing witnesses of the unending story. Continue to write your words within our hearts, that we may become the storytellers for the next generation.

We pray this in Christ's name. Amen.

ENRICHING THE EXPERIENCE

In addition to the six regular sessions of Faith Talk, consider having one or more special sessions, using one of the following activities.

1. Hold a "Trinity" dinner

Using your best creativity, hold a special dinner, using the Trinity as a theme for the meal. How many dishes can you dream up that have at least three distinct ingredients in one dish? Perhaps you might have bacon, lettuce, and tomato sandwiches, with a three-layered gelatin salad. For dessert, you might choose a three-scoop sundae with three different toppings. Use your imagination, and enjoy a time of fellowship.

2. Watch a video

Have a video night. Choose a movie that will build on the theme of one or more of the sessions. Be sure to follow copyright regulations in showing a video—an informal showing in someone's home is less likely to be a violation than a showing in church, which can be considered a "public" presentation. Some choices might be:

- *As Good as it Gets,* to look at the human condition.
- *The Gods Must Be Crazy*, where a soft drink bottle falling from an airplane disrupts the worldview of an African tribe.
- *Grand Canyon,* for a discussion of evil and good in the midst of chaos.
- *Jesus Christ, Superstar, The Last Temptation of Christ,* or another movie focusing on the life of Christ.
- *Field of Dreams,* for a discussion of how the Holy Spirit might work.
- *The Apostle,* about a traveling evangelist who is in love with God's Spirit but also filled with many human failings.
- *Leap of Faith,* about what happens when a charlatan faith healer actually experiences a miracle.
- *Spitfire Grill,* a small-town tale where a woman ex-con brings redemption to a New England community.

Enjoy a light dessert or snack after the video while discussing how the movie relates to themes covered in this course.

3. Visit another church

Visit a worship service for another denomination. Select one that is very different from your own. Note how images of God, Jesus, and the Holy Spirit are portrayed in the architecture, worship symbols, stained glass windows, liturgy, and music. How is it alike? different? Are any new images suggested? Consider visiting a Jewish synagogue. Obviously, images of Jesus will not be present, but how is God portrayed? Seeing God through the eyes of another religion can expand our own view.

4. Review a book

If the group was particularly interested in one or more of the themes, consider doing further study through a book review or book study. Your pastor or representatives at Christian Board of Publication should be able to recommend current books that focus on any of these issues.

5. Visit an exhibit of religious art

Check the museums in your own or nearby communities for showings of traditional or contemporary religious art. What new insights do the visual representations of a greater reality bring? Or, use the Internet and have a "field trip" in cyberspace. Many museums and the Vatican itself can be accessed and their artwork viewed. This will take some homework on someone's part to search for the sites but can be an extremely worthwhile experience.

A QUICK BIBLE ROAD MAP

People who are new to Bible study may find it intimidating (not to mention confusing) when someone instructs, "Look up Deuteronomy 6:4." Sometimes you get lucky, thumbing through and skimming the book titles at the top of the pages. Deuteronomy is a big book, and it's near the beginning of the Bible. But if the reference is to a shorter book somewhere in the middle, that system breaks down.

Referring to page numbers doesn't help, because different sizes and versions of the Bible number pages differently. So we're stuck with referring to passages by book, chapter, and verse.

Here are some clues to make the search easier.

1. Use the table of contents, if you don't know the order of books. Remember that the Bible has two sections, the Old Testament and New Testament. They are listed separately in the table of contents, and most often each testament starts on its own page 1. Skim down the list until you find the right book, go to the page number and find the chapter, then the verse. Some Bibles offer an alphabetical index to the books of the Bible after the table of contents.

2. Remember that each Testament is organized in its own way. In Protestant Bibles, the order is like this:

   Old Testament

   Stories of God's People (Genesis—Esther)
   Songs and Wisdom Literature (Job—Song of Solomon)
   Prophets (Isaiah—Malachi)

   New Testament

   Stories about Jesus (Matthew—John)
   Stories of the Early Church (Acts)
   Letters to Churches and Their Leaders (Romans—Jude)
   Prophet (Revelation)

3. If your Bible doesn't contain the Apocrypha, here's another method of finding your way around. Open your Bible to the middle. Most often, you will come to the Psalms, the longest book of the Bible. Open the second half of the Bible to the middle, and you will come either to the very end of the Old Testament or to the Gospels at the beginning of the New Testament.

4. Practice. When you read an article at home that has biblical references, look them up! It will help you become familiar with the Bible as a whole.

5. Decode the punctuation marks. In the Bible, chapter numbers are usually large and verse numbers tiny. When some other book or article refers to a passage in the Bible, it gives the book name first, then the chapter, then (usually after a colon) the verse or verses. That isn't too bad. Book—chapter—colon—verse. But longer references can be confusing.

A little dash means "through." Matthew 5:1–8 means Matthew chapter five, verses 1 *through* 8.

A comma separates two passages in the same chapter. Matthew 5:1–8, 12–15 refers to verses 1 through 8 and 12 through 15.

A semicolon separates passages in separate chapters or books. Genesis 1:1–4; 2:3–5; John 1:1–4 points to passages in two chapters of Genesis and one in the Gospel of John.

A long dash also means "through," but it shows that a passage extends over two or more chapters. 1 Corinthians 12:27—14:5 contains the last part of chapter 12, all of 13, and the first 5 verses of chapter 14.

When there is no colon after a chapter number, the reference is to a whole chapter. Psalm 8. Luke 15.

Small letters after a verse reference give you a clue that the verse has been subdivided into natural sections—usually sentences or phrases. Genesis 1:1—2:4a contains one account of the creation. A second account begins at 2:4b. Look it up and you'll find that most Bibles have a paragraph break there. Genesis 1:4a, though, runs to the semicolon.

6. There are other tricks to finding your way around in the Bible. Some people buy index tabs that show where each book begins. If you have a study Bible, become familiar with the extra information it offers. Some study Bibles have lists of important passages or favorite stories, so you can, for example, find the Ten Commandments quickly, without skimming the whole book of Deuteronomy.

7. As you read different parts of the Bible, don't be afraid to use a pencil, pen, or highlighter to mark important passages. Put a star or exclamation mark by passages that have a special impact on you. Or note what a passage is about, if your Bible doesn't have its own notations. Then when you skim the pages of your Bible, you can easily rediscover some treasures that otherwise could be buried.

LOOK FOR THESE FAITH CROSSINGS TITLES:

Available now:

God's Ordinary People—A look at some fascinating but little-known biblical characters.

Faith Talk—An introduction to basic Christian beliefs.

Following God into the Future—As we welcome a new millennium, where will our faith journeys take us?

Available December 1998:

Through the Fire—A Bible study on facing tough times.

ABC's of the Bible—Twenty-six key verses draw us into the fascinating world of the scripture.

Show No Partiality—A lively dialogue on facing the challenge of racism.

Available June 1999:

Living Water—Take the plunge—explore the rich symbolism of water in the Bible!

Worship—the Whys, Whats, and Hows—Explore vital questions about what it means to worship God.

When Christ and Caesar Meet—Never discuss religion and politics? This course takes on both!

And even more fascinating FAITH CROSSINGS courses are in the works!

To Order: Call Christian Board at 1-800-366-3383. Visit our Web site: www.cbp21.com